GW01398871

thirsty earth

Exploring the Science of Droughts

sarah michaels

contents

introduction

what is a drought?

Can you picture throwing the biggest water balloon fight on the block? All your friends are invited, the bright sun is beaming, and your backyard is covered with dozens of fun water balloons. Just as everyone is ready to start splashing, though, you turn on the water spigot. But, oh no! Only a tiny stream trickles out.

You fumble with the knob, but no matter how hard you turn, there still isn't enough water to fill one water balloon. Imagine throwing the biggest water balloon fight on the block, but the water never comes. What a bummer, huh? That's sort of what happens during a drought. A drought occurs when our huge, amazing planet has water troubles. Over the course of a few days, weeks, or even years, the water simply runs out.

The Earth's Water Supply

Understanding How Dry Seasons Work Now that we have an idea of where droughts happen the most, let's consider the Earth's water supply. Water on Earth is in a continuous cycle. The water cycle is the way nature recycles water. You learned about it a little while ago. The water cycle keeps our lakes, rivers and under-the-ground water supplies filled.

What Exactly is a Drought?

But sometimes, the cycle gets a bit unbalanced. A drought happens when an area doesn't get enough water for an extended period of time. It's not just about not enough rain on any particular hot, sunny day — a drought means not enough water, for a long, long time Imagine if the water fountain in the schoolyard wasn't big enough to give even a sip of water to all the kids out on the playground during lunch hour, except that "lunch hour" actually lasted for weeks or months. That's the situation plenty of places around the world are in right now.

Why Should We Care?

You may be wondering why droughts are a problem. I mean, they happen anyway, right? The thing is, when droughts hit, they can impact everything around us. All plants and animals need water. Without it, their lives can be pretty tough. Crops might not grow as well. That means less food in the shops and often more expensive food too. Similarly, when rivers and lakes dry up, there is less water for us to have at home for drinking, cooking and yes, having fun.

Water, Water, Not Everywhere

During a drought, it might seem like the water has all but gone, when in truth it's just not in all the usual places. Below the surface, there are areas called aquifers, which are sort of like huge underground lakes. We get a lot of our water from these places, and they don't refill quickly enough during a drought to replace what we've taken from them and consumed. This is an issue, of course, for all living creatures, not just people.

The Sneaky Slow Down

One of the tricky things about droughts is that they can sneak up on us. They start slowly, and sometimes people don't notice the signs until water levels are already quite low. It's like when you're so caught up in playing or watching TV that you don't realize how late it has gotten. By the time you notice, it's already way past bedtime!

Joining Hands with Nature

Even though we can't cause end to drought, we can help during drier times out to conserve water. We need to take care of water usage so that it is available to all. Small efforts of turning off the tap while brushing the teeth are necessary. We can also plant low water consumption plants in the garden. Small efforts can be beneficial.

Every Drop Counts

It's true, every drop of water counts. Droughts are definitely not a favorite for most of us, but if we are to understand what causes these dry spells as well as how we can prevent them, we could each become water-saving superheroes. Picture it like this, as a player on a sports team, you matter. You belong, but you also have to contribute. Well, the game of water is just the same. Every drop counts!

Keep Learning and Exploring

By coming to understand droughts, it makes us all the more thankful for our water and helps instill awareness in us about how we all exactly need to treat our planet. We're not just talking about today but we should also be making sure that there will be enough tomorrow and the day after that.

brief overview of why understanding droughts is important

Why do some things matter so much? Why do you have to learn how to tie your shoes or have to brush your teeth every day? Droughts are a little bit like that. They are really important, and today we are going to figure out why.

Water Is Life!

First off, water is essential for all life on Earth. You, me, plants, animals, and even tiny bugs we can barely see— all of us need water to live. When there's a drought, it means water is scarce, and that can make things really tough for everyone and everything.

Farms Need Water Too

Imagine you're a farmer who grows crops like corn, wheat, and vegetables. What do you think would happen if it didn't rain enough? Yep, you guessed it— without enough water, the plants wouldn't grow well, and there might not be enough food to go around. Farmers rely on regular weather patterns to grow food, and when droughts mess with these patterns, it can lead to less food and sometimes even higher prices in stores. That affects what your family can buy when they go shopping.

Water for Cities and Towns

It's not just farms that need water; cities and towns do too. Water is used for so many things in our daily lives, from cooking and cleaning to putting out fires and keeping public swimming pools full. When there's a drought, water isn't as plentiful, and that can mean a lot of changes to how we use it every day. Sometimes, towns even have to make rules about using less water—like not watering lawns or washing cars—to make sure there's enough to go around.

Nature's Balancing Act

Droughts can also affect the environment in big ways. Rivers, lakes, and wetlands can get smaller or even dry up, which is tough on the fish and animals that live there. They depend on these water bodies for their habitat and food. When their homes are in trouble, it affects the whole ecosystem. That's the big network of living things and their environment, all depending on each other to thrive.

The Weather Connection

Droughts can influence weather too. When the ground is dry, it soaks up heat faster than when it is wet. Some of this extra heat is used to evaporate water into the atmosphere. But a lot of it just makes the ground hotter. Those hot surface temperatures can make a drought even worse. Less rainfall makes the ground drier, which makes temperatures hotter and the drought deeper. And the cycle continues.

Why We All Need to Be Water-Smart

Understanding droughts helps us get better at using water wisely. We all need to be water-smart, which means knowing how to save water even when there isn't a drought. This helps make sure there's enough water to go around, whether we're in a dry spell or not. Being water-smart can include simple things like turning off the tap while you brush your teeth or choosing a shorter shower instead of a bath.

Scientists Are on the Case

Scientists work hard to study droughts, predict when they'll happen, and figure out the best ways to manage water. By understanding what causes droughts and how they affect us, scientists can help farmers, city planners, and even government leaders make smart decisions about water use. This kind of teamwork helps everyone be better prepared when a drought happens.

Learning Today for a Better Tomorrow

The more you know about drought, the better prepared you will be in the future. Knowledge is like a tool in your tool box. The more tools you have, the better you can build or fix anything. By learning about drought, you gain an important tool that will allow you to make smart decisions about water use and to help explain why it is important to be water-wise.

1 /
the water cycle

THE AMAZING JOURNEY OF WATER:
Understanding the Water Cycle

Do you ever wonder where the glass of water you drink comes from? Or the rain that pours from the sky during a thunderstorm? Is it magic? Well, it's not magic! It's the water cycle! We are going to search for water. We have to play detective and find out how water travels all over the Earth. Get your magnifying glasses and let's go!

Step 1: Evaporation - The Great Escape

First up on our water cycle journey is evaporation. Think of it as water's way of going on a sky adventure. When the sun shines down on bodies of water like oceans, lakes, and even puddles, it heats up the water. As the water gets warmer, it turns into vapor or steam and rises up into the air. This is evaporation!

But it's not just large bodies of water that give off vapor. Plants also join in the fun through a process called transpiration. Just like you sweat on a hot day, plants release water vapor from their leaves into the air. So every time you see plants and trees, remember, they're little water cycle helpers!

Step 2: Condensation - Cloud Building

As the water vapor rises higher into the sky, it starts to cool down. This is where condensation comes into play. Condensation is like a giant gathering where all the water vapor cools off and comes together. As the vapor cools, it changes back into tiny droplets of liquid water, forming clouds. You can think of clouds as floating water parties!

. . .

Have you ever noticed how the mirror fogs up after a hot shower? That's condensation in action! The steam from your shower cools down when it hits the cooler mirror, turning back into tiny drops of water. That's exactly what happens up in the sky to form clouds.

Step 3: Precipitation - The Big Drop

Now that our clouds are all loaded up with water, what happens next? It's time for precipitation! This is the part where water makes its dramatic entrance back to Earth. Depending on the temperature, it might fall as rain, snow, sleet, or hail.

Rain comes down when the cloud droplets combine and get too heavy to stay up in the air. Snow happens when the air up high is so cold that the water vapor turns directly into ice crystals, which stick together and fall as snowflakes. Whether it's a gentle sprinkle or a blizzard, it's all part of the water's return journey to the ground.

. . .

Step 4: Collection - Water's Gathering

Once the water hits the ground, it begins what we call the collection stage. This is where water gathers back into lakes, rivers, oceans, and even underground. From there, it soaks into the soil, replenishing Earth and giving life to plants. Some of it travels deep underground to become part of aquifers—giant stores of groundwater that people all over the world rely on for their water supply.

But the journey doesn't end there! Some of this water will evaporate again, starting the whole cycle over. It's a never-ending adventure for every drop of water, constantly moving and changing form.

Water All Around Us

But consider this: the water you drank today might have started life as snow on a mountain or been part of an ocean on the other side of the planet. Perhaps it flowed in a river or became part of a cloud. In prehistoric times, it might even have been taken up by a dinosaur to quench its thirst! Water connects each of us with pieces of the whole planet and with every moment in history.

Understanding the water cycle makes us appreciate how vitally important every drop is. We know that every drop we use washes back and forth between the Earth and the sky. As the water cycle turns, everything in it is reused over and over, which is why it is so important to keep water clean and not to waste it. We must use it thoughtfully and treat it with care. Then, the water cycle will continue to support life on Earth as it always has.

Let's Be Water Wise

It is clear that water has quite an amazing journey. It takes many highways and byways and shortcuts all across the world! But our water's journey is much like an adventure story. And like any good adventure story, each character or each and every drop of water is important to the water cycle story. That is why we all need to be very careful about how we waste or use water. You can help by making sure you do not let water run while you brush your teeth. It is really amazing how much water you waste if you let it run while you are brushing your teeth. You can also help by fixing a faucet that is leaking. You might think that a few drops don't matter, but actually, they do. Every little bit of water conservation helps!

simple experiments to visualize each part of the water cycle

Did you ever wish you could be a magician? To create something very cool right there at home? Well, today, you will be a cross between a scientist and magician. Together we are going to do some exciting experiments. And you will see part of the water cycle happening! Sound like fun? Well come along and begin our water magic!

Experiment 1: Capturing Evaporation

Materials Needed:

- A clear plastic cup
- Water
- A marker
- A warm place like a sunny window

What to Do:

1. Fill the plastic cup about halfway with water.
2. Use the marker to draw a line at the water level.
3. Place the cup in a sunny window and observe what happens over a few days.

· · ·

What's Happening:

This experiment shows evaporation, which is the first part of the water cycle. The heat from the sun (or the warmth of the room) makes the water slowly turn into vapor and rise into the air. You'll notice that the water level in the cup goes down. This disappearing act is the water vaporizing, just like it does in lakes and oceans!

Experiment 2: Forming Condensation

Materials Needed:
- A metal can or a glass
- Ice cubes
- A room-temperature room

What to Do:
1. Fill the can or glass with ice cubes.
2. Watch the outside of the can or glass for a few minutes.

What's Happening:

Condensation is the star of this show! As you watch, you'll see water droplets forming on the outside of the can or glass. This happens because the cold surface cools the air around it. Water vapor in the warm air cools down when it touches the cold surface and turns back into liquid, forming droplets. It's just like how clouds form from water vapor in the sky!

Experiment 3: Making Rain with Precipitation

Materials Needed:
- A large clear plastic container with a lid
- A small cup
- Hot water
- Ice cubes

What to Do:

1. Pour hot water into the large container until it's about an inch deep.

2. Place the small cup in the center of the large container. Make sure it doesn't get wet inside.

3. Quickly cover the large container with its lid.

4. Put ice cubes on top of the lid.

5. Watch what happens inside the container for a few minutes.

· · ·

What's Happening:

This experiment is like a mini weather system! The hot water in the container creates warm, moist air by evaporation. When this moist air rises and hits the cold lid (cooled by the ice), it condenses into water droplets. These droplets collect and get heavier, and eventually, they fall back into the large container like rain. You've just made it rain indoors!

Experiment 4: Observing Collection

Materials Needed:
- A sponge
- Water
- A plate

What to Do:

1. Soak the sponge in water and place it on the plate.

2. Observe what happens when you leave the sponge for a while.

What's Happening:

In this simple setup, the sponge acts like the ground

or a body of water. When you soak the sponge, it collects water just like land collects rainwater in lakes, rivers, or underground. As time goes on, some of the water might evaporate back into the air, and the cycle would start all over again if we continued to observe.

Let's Talk Science

Each of these experiments helps us see parts of the water cycle up close. By doing these, you're not just having fun; you're also learning how the real world works around you. The water cycle is happening all the time, everywhere—even if we can't see it with our own eyes.

2 /
what causes a drought?

WHY DO DROUGHTS HAPPEN?

Ever wondered why some places are wet while others can be bone dry for months, or even years? Sometimes it seems like nature has an unfair remote control that just won't press the "rain" button. So, how does drought happen? Today we're going to explore this topic, so get ready to don your intrepid explorer hat. We think you're going to find this fascinating.

When Rain Takes a Break

The simplest explanation for a drought, and the one many of us know, is that it doesn't rain. Just like you can have a day where you don't feel like doing much, you can have a day where the weather can't be bothered to rain. This doesn't tend to be because the weather is feeling lazy, though, but rather because of the wind patterns in the atmosphere.

The reason it doesn't rain a lot in the desert is a simple one: the winds push the clouds away. And if there aren't clouds, there can't be rain. Another way of looking at this is a drought is simply a prolonged period of abnormally low rainfall; and like any garden, if yours doesn't see much rain for a few weeks, it starts to look just as thirsty. Similarly, the ground, rivers, and lakes won't receive enough water, and will virtually dry up.

Climate Change: Turning Up the Heat

If global warming is like turning up the heat in a big oven, climate change is like shaking up a global soda-pop bottle. If global warming is the heat, climate change is the thing that happens when things really start to fizz. In other words, as the Earth gets hotter, it changes weather patterns all around the world. And sometimes those patterns can make droughts happen more or worse.

So think of a drought as summer vacation—the longer, the better, right? Not always. Sort of, but in reverse. The normal patterns for summer are getting stretched out and in the wrong places. So that means, in some places, there's longer and more rain, and others there's not enough rain.

Too Much Watering: When Humans Use Too Much Water

Now, let's talk about another big reason for droughts: us! Yes, human activities can actually cause droughts. When we use too much water—for farms, factories, and even our homes—it can take away from the natural sources like rivers, lakes, and underground reservoirs. This is kind of like when everyone wants a piece of your birthday cake. If too many friends help themselves, there might not be enough left for you!

One of the biggest water users is agriculture. To grow food, farmers need a lot of water, but if they use too much, there might not be enough to go around. It's a delicate balance. Keeping enough water in the ground and in our rivers is crucial, not just for people, but for animals and plants too.

What Happens Next?

. . .

All of these different reasons-no rain, changing weather patterns and too much water being taken out by humans-can lead to a drought. It is a little bit like when you are doing a jigsaw puzzle, you need all the pieces to make the full picture. If one piece is missing the picture, or in this case the drought, will not be complete.

By learning about all these different pieces, such as droughts, we can help get a clearer picture of what is happening. Scientists and people who make the decisions, like the government and councils, use this information to help to make sure that there is enough water for people and plants in the future. Now that we know how droughts happen we can start thinking about what we can do to help. Whether it is by using less water at home, or joining in with other people in community efforts to use less water, every little bit helps and everyone can do something.

3 /
types of drought

THE CASE of the Missing Rain: Understanding Meteorological Drought

Have you ever had a week or two of beautiful weather and sunshine and thought it would be that way forever? You may have spent the time outside with picnics and games, not even thinking about the rain. But if you were a farmer or gardener, you might have been getting worried. If the stretch of nice weather and sunshine keeps going, and going, and going and you never see a raindrop, we need to start talking about a drought! Not all droughts are the same, you know. Meteorological drought is the kind of drought that happens when it simply doesn't rain enough. Keep reading, and we think you will start to get the picture!

When the Weather Decides Not to Rain

Meteorological drought happens when an area gets

much less rain than usual for a long period. This isn't just about missing a day or two of rain; it's about weeks, months, or sometimes even longer when the weather patterns just don't bring in those water-packed clouds.

You see, the weather is like a big puzzle, with pieces like wind, air pressure, temperature, and moisture all coming together to decide if it will rain, snow, or stay dry. During a meteorological drought, the pieces of this puzzle line up in a way that keeps the rain away.

The Wind's Role in Our Weather Story

Let's talk about the wind for a moment. Wind plays a huge part in our weather. There are certain wind patterns that can push clouds filled with rain away from an area. For instance, if winds blow from a direction that usually has dry air, they can keep the moist, rainy clouds at bay. It's like the wind is a big broom, sweeping the clouds away before they can drop any rain.

High Pressure: The Invisible Shield

Another piece of the puzzle is high pressure areas. These are parts of the atmosphere where the air pressure is higher than the areas around them. High pressure acts like an invisible shield in the sky. It pushes air down, which stops clouds from forming and growing. Without clouds, the rain can't form, and the skies stay clear. This high pressure is one of the main reasons some places have long periods without rain.

The Sun Heats Things Up

Temperature also plays a big role. When an area has higher temperatures, it can worsen a drought. How? Well, warmer air can hold more moisture, so even if there is some water around, the air might suck it up and keep it from turning into rain. Plus, warmer temperatures make water evaporate faster from soil and plants. This means the ground and vegetation get drier, quicker.

What This Means for People and the Planet

When meteorological droughts happen, they can

lead to a lot of challenges. Farmers might have trouble growing crops because there's not enough water. Wildlife that depends on water sources like ponds and rivers might find their homes shrinking or disappearing. And people in towns and cities might have to start using less water to make sure there's enough to go around.

Observing the Signs

Scientists keep an eye on the weather to help predict when and where a drought might happen. They use tools like satellites to watch cloud patterns and measure temperatures and wind. They also study the history of the weather in different places to understand the patterns that lead to droughts. This helps them warn people ahead of time so they can prepare.

Every Bit of Knowledge Helps

Understanding how meteorological droughts work helps us all be better prepared. If we know that a dry spell is coming, farmers can plan what kinds of crops to plant, cities can manage their water use, and everyone can do their part to conserve water.

Let's Be Weather Detectives

So now you know a little bit about meteorological droughts! You can be a weather detective too. Check out the weather report and take a look at the sky yourself. What is the wind like? Which direction is it coming from? Is the sky full of clouds, or can you see for miles?

All these things can help you spot the weather patterns you expect.

The Puzzle of Thirsty Fields: Understanding Agricultural Drought

It's fascinating how something as small as a seed can grow into a plant that provides food. But what happens when these plants are not watered? This is an agricultural drought. Read on to learn how an agricultural drought can affect everything from the soil beneath you to the food on your table.

What is Agricultural Drought?

Agricultural drought happens when there isn't enough water for crops to grow properly. It's not just about it being sunny for a few days. This type of drought can last for weeks or months, leaving the soil so dry that plants struggle to survive and grow.

The Soil Story

The story begins with the soil. Soil isn't just dirt—it's a living thing full of nutrients, tiny organisms, and, yes, water! Plants depend on moist soil for their roots to absorb water and the nutrients they need to grow. When the soil dries out because there isn't enough rain or irrigation, it becomes hard and compact. This makes it tough for roots to spread out, and they can't access the deeper moisture they rely on during dry spells.

The Sun and Wind: Not Always Helpful

You might think the sun and wind are always good

for plants, but during a drought, they can actually make things worse. The sun heats up the soil, speeding up evaporation—the process where water turns into vapor and escapes into the air. Wind can whisk away the moisture even faster. It's like when you feel thirsty on a hot, windy day at the beach; the plants feel the same way!

The Ripple Effects on Farms

When crops don't get enough water, they can't grow as big or as healthy as they should. This means farmers have smaller harvests and sometimes even lose entire fields of crops. It's not just bad news for the farmers—it affects all of us. Fewer crops mean less food in the stores and often higher prices. It can also mean that farmers have to make tough choices about using more water to try to save their crops or planting different kinds that might not need as much water.

How Farmers Fight Back

Farmers are pretty clever when it comes to fighting agricultural drought. Here are a few tricks they have up their sleeves:

- Irrigation: This is like giving the plants a drink with a hose instead of waiting for rain. Farmers use different systems to get water to their crops, like sprinklers, drips, or even recycling water.

- Choosing the Right Crops: Some plants are better at handling drought than others. Farmers might plant these drought-tolerant varieties to make sure they can grow something, even when water is scarce.

- Mulching: Farmers cover the soil with mulch—a layer of material like straw or leaves—to help keep moisture in the soil. It's like putting a lid on a pot to stop the steam from escaping.

- Conservation Tillage: This method involves leaving some of the previous crop's remains on the field to help protect the soil from the sun and wind, which helps keep more moisture in the soil.

Every Drop Counts

Conserving water isn't just for farmers—it's important for all of us. By understanding how tough it is for plants to grow during a drought, we can all appreciate the value of water. Simple things you can do at home, like turning off the tap while brushing your teeth or using water-wise plants in your garden, help make sure there's enough water to go around.

Keep Growing Your Knowledge

Agricultural drought is a great example of how the complications of the world around us are just nature doing what nature does. Farming and water and soil and plants and even the weather are all part of one, big interconnected system, and if one part of the system is having trouble, like not enough rain, then it affects everything around it.

Now that you know more, start thinking about things

you can do to help! You might not be a farmer, but you could be a scientist who discovers new ways to grow plants, or an engineer who invents better ways to save water. Maybe you will teach your family and friends about how to help too!

The Mystery of the Vanishing Rivers: Understanding Hydrological Drought

We've all probably seen it: a river that's roaring high and fast, with water splashing over rocks or within a riverbed deeply filled with water. And if you returned to the river on another occasion, maybe a few months later, there is either just a trickle, or even no water at all. That's a hydrological drought. So, let's float down this watery mystery and learn what happens: when rivers, lakes, and even underground water levels become too low.

What is Hydrological Drought?

Hydrological drought occurs when the water supply in natural sources like rivers, lakes, and groundwater becomes significantly lower than usual. It can happen because of many reasons, which all trace back to not having enough rain over a long period or other changes that reduce water levels.

Rivers and Lakes: The Earth's Water Collection

Rivers and lakes are like Earth's own water collection system. They gather water from rainfall and from streams that flow down mountains and hills. They're important because they supply water for drinking, farming, and keeping our natural ecosystems healthy. But what happens when there isn't enough rain to keep them filled?

The Slow Disappearance

Imagine filling a bathtub with water, then pulling the plug while continuing to add just a little water at a time. Eventually, the water level starts to drop. This is similar to what happens during a hydrological drought. Rainfall might continue, but if it's not enough to replace what's lost through evaporation and use, the water level in rivers and lakes starts to fall.

The Sun and Wind Team Up Again

Just like in agricultural drought, the sun and wind are major players in hydrological drought. The sun heats up the water, causing it to evaporate—turn into vapor—and the wind can blow this vapor away from the surface. If the weather stays hot and windy for a long time without enough rain, lakes and rivers can begin to shrink faster than they can be refilled.

Groundwater: The Hidden Water Source

Beneath the Earth's surface, there are layers of soil and rock that hold water—this is called groundwater. In many places, people rely on this groundwater for their water supply, especially when rivers and lakes are low. However, during a hydrological drought, groundwater levels can also drop. This happens because there isn't enough rain to seep into the ground and refill these underground reserves.

The Impact on Wildlife and Humans

Hydrological drought doesn't just affect people; it also impacts wildlife. Fish, birds, and animals that depend on rivers and lakes for food and water can find themselves in trouble when these water bodies dry up. For people, a lower water supply means there might not be enough water for drinking, growing food, or even producing electricity in places that rely on hydroelectric power from rivers.

Watching the Water Levels

Scientists and environmentalists keep an eye on water levels in rivers and lakes to help predict hydrological droughts. They use tools like satellites to measure how much water is in these bodies and sensors to monitor groundwater levels. This information can help communities prepare for dry periods by conserving water and planning how to use the water they have wisely.

What Can We Do?

Even though it might seem like a big problem, there are ways to tackle hydrological drought. Saving water at home, like taking shorter showers and fixing leaks, helps reduce the demand on water supplies. Communities can also protect wetlands and forests that help store and regulate water flow, ensuring there's more water in the system during dry times.

When There's Not Enough Water to Go Around: Exploring Socioeconomic Drought

Picture this: you're throwing a big picnic, and you want to make lemonade. You have tons of sugar and bags of lemons ready to go, but not much water. What are you going to do? You'll have to figure out how to make it work with the water you have, right? That problem is like a socioeconomic drought. A socioeconomic drought occurs when we don't have enough water to meet the needs of people, farms, and factories. In the following activity, we'll go through the interpretation of a graph to see what happens when the demand for water exceeds the supply.

What is Socioeconomic Drought?

Socioeconomic drought occurs when the water available in rivers, lakes, and reservoirs isn't enough to fulfill the needs of a population and its economy. This type of drought is about more than just dry weather; it's about how the shortage of water affects everyone and everything that depends on it.

Water, Water Everywhere, But Not Enough to Drink

In cities and towns, people need water for drinking, cooking, and cleaning. Businesses need it to make products and run their operations. Farmers need it to irrigate crops. When there isn't enough to go around, it can lead to some serious challenges. Water becomes a precious commodity, and managing it wisely becomes more important than ever.

The Balancing Act of Water Use

Managing water during a socioeconomic drought is like balancing a seesaw. On one side, you have the natural supply of water from rain and reservoirs. On the other side, you have everyone's needs pulling it down, trying to get enough water. When one side is much heavier than the other, it can cause problems.

Cities might have to impose water restrictions, which means people are only allowed to use water for essential activities. Farmers might receive less water for irrigation, which can affect the amount of food they grow. This can lead to smaller harvests and even affect food prices at your local grocery store!

The Ripple Effects on the Community

When water is scarce, it doesn't just affect how much you can drink or use at home. It can lead to bigger issues in the community. Parks and public gardens might not get watered, affecting outdoor spaces where people relax and play. In extreme cases, businesses that use a lot of water might have to slow down production, which can lead to people working fewer hours or not having jobs.

How Communities Respond

Different places have different ways of dealing with socioeconomic drought. Some cities invest in technology to recycle water, making every drop count more than once. Others might set up programs to encourage people to use less water, like offering rebates for installing water-efficient appliances.

Education plays a big role, too. Schools and community centers might host workshops to teach people how to save water, like using a bucket to catch rainwater for watering plants or fixing leaky faucets to prevent wasting water.

Learning from the Challenges

Every challenge brings a lesson, and socioeconomic drought teaches us a lot about the value of water. By seeing firsthand how tough things can get when water is limited, communities learn to appreciate and conserve this vital resource. It shows us that every little action, like turning off the tap while brushing your teeth, adds up to big savings on water.

The Power of Working Together

One of the coolest things about facing challenges like socioeconomic drought is seeing how people come together to solve problems. Neighbors, schools, businesses, and governments all have to work together to make sure there's enough water to go around. It's a powerful reminder of how connected we all are and how everyone's actions can make a difference.

4 /
the effects of drought

THE THIRSTY FOREST: A Tale of Plants and Animals in a Drought

Ever wonder what happens to plants and animals when it doesn't rain for weeks or even months? Climb into this book and find out! Have you ever seen the rain? Not a drop to drink. Come on an ecological adventure into the fascinating world of drought. Find out why it's so hard for plants and animals in the forest when water disappears in this story, based on real events.

The River's Whisper

Once upon a time in a green, healthy forest, the river was the pulse of life. It was deep and clear, and all of the forest creatures, small and large, relied on it. It was on the banks of the river that the birds sang in the trees, and the deer roamed and snacked. The fish danced through the river's cool, clean waters. But as the weeks passed and the months filled with dryness, there was no rain. The river started to whisper. It was getting weak.

In this lush and lively forest, Rina the red fox loved to play in the river. She would jump and splash in the crisp, flowing water. One day Rina the red fox saw that the river had shrunk, and all that was left was a little stream. It was almost empty of fish and the banks were dry and cracked.

The Wilted Banquet

Near the river stood an ancient oak tree named Old Barky, whose roots stretched deep and wide. Old Barky had seen many seasons, but this drought was harsher than any he remembered. His leaves turned from a vibrant green to a tired brown. "I need a drink to keep my leaves dancing," he would rustle in the wind.

Beneath Old Barky, Bella the butterfly flitted from flower to flower. But each flower held less nectar, their petals drooping sadly. "Where have all the sweet waters gone?" Bella wondered as she searched for food.

The Drying Den

Rina's den, cozy and hidden beneath the roots of a large willow, was feeling the drought too. The soil around it had hardened, and the cool dampness that once seeped from the river was now a distant memory. Food was becoming scarce as well, as the mice and rabbits she hunted struggled to find their own meals in the drying underbrush.

One evening, Rina sat by her shrinking water hole, her thoughts troubled by the changes. "How can I help bring the forest back to life?" she pondered, her eyes reflecting the fading stars.

The Gathering

Determined, Rina called a meeting with all the forest dwellers. They gathered in the moonlight, where the river once sang the loudest. Old Barky shared stories of the old waters, Bella spoke of the shrinking flowers, and even Leo, the lazy lizard, complained about the hot rocks no longer cooled by the river's mist.

Together, they decided to venture farther into the forest, to find help or perhaps discover a hidden spring that Old Barky recalled from the tales of his sapling days.

. . .

The Journey for Water

The next morning, with the sun climbing, Rina led the way. They trekked through the forest, over dry leaves that crunched underfoot and past bushes that once teemed with berries now barren. After what felt like a lifetime, the group reached a hill that overlooked a hidden valley.

There, to their wonder, was a small pond, cradled by ancient rocks, its waters clear and inviting. "The hidden spring! It's real!" Bella exclaimed, fluttering excitedly.

New Beginnings

The animals drank deeply, splashed joyfully, and filled their bellies. Rina, with help from the others, dug a small channel from the pond back toward their home, hoping to redirect some water to revive their drying land.

Over time, the new water channel helped. Though the river was not as full as before, there was enough moisture to keep the plants alive and the animals happy. Old Barky's leaves began to dance again, and Bella's flowers bloomed with renewed vigor.

Lessons from the Forest

In the forest, life gradually returned. The animals began to conserve water, treating every drop that reached their land from the secret spring as precious. Rina sat by the stream often, looking over her home and feeling proud of it as the forest recovered, and of the part that all of the animals had played in it.

impact on humans

Imagine turning on the kitchen tap and not a drop of water comes out. Or going to the grocery store and discovering there are no more apples, oranges, or asparagus. This is not only a made-up story, but a reality many people around the world are faced with during a drought. We will also see how drought can hurt the people in our lives through water shortage, food not being available, and in our wallet.

The Thirsty Town

· · ·

Once upon a time there was a very small town. Everyone who lived there knew everyone else. In the town there was a river. In summertime, everyone loved to go fishing in the river and to swim, canoe, and waterski on its waters. The thirsty forest and river friends The townspeople also relied on the river for all of their practical needs such as drinking, cooking and washing.

But one dry summer, the town found itself in the same situation as the thirsty forest. The river started to dry up. There was not enough water for everyone who lived in the town. And lack of water affected most every part of life. Lawn turned brown. Gardens would not grow. People were only allowed to use a certain amount of water every few days at home. Washing cars, filling swimming pools, and other things that needed water became difficult to do or a luxury that was always questioned.

The Vanishing Harvests

With the river low and fields drying out, the local farmers struggle. Crops like corn and tomatoes start to wilt and wither under the scorching sun. Without enough water, plants can't grow properly, and the farmers face a tough season.

. . .

This leads to food shortages. At the local market, shelves once filled with fresh produce are now sparse. Prices for fruits and vegetables go up, making it harder for families to fill their shopping carts with healthy food. Kids might notice that their favorite snacks, like apples and oranges, are not as plentiful or as juicy as they were before.

Money Matters

The lack of water doesn't just mean you can't wash your car or water your lawn; it also starts to affect the town's economy. Let's look at how this happens. First, farmers earn less money because they grow fewer crops. This means they have less to spend in local stores.

Businesses that rely on water, like car washes and landscapers, also earn less because they can't operate as usual. Even restaurants and cafes might feel the pinch, as they use lots of water for cooking and cleaning. When these businesses earn less, they might have to reduce hours or even let some of their workers go.

· · ·

As people spend less, the town's economy slows down. This can make things tough for everyone, from the shop owners to the families who live there.

Together We Can

In our story about the thirsty forest, the animals worked together to find a solution. People can do the same! In times of drought, communities come together to save water and help each other. Here are some ways they might do this:

- Water-Saving Programs: Towns might start programs that encourage people to use less water, like fixing leaks or using water-efficient appliances.
    - Community Gardens: These are special areas where people grow fruits and vegetables together. By sharing resources, they can grow more with less water.
    - Education: Schools and community groups teach everyone from kids to adults about the importance of saving water and how to do it effectively.

Looking Ahead

. . .

As with any problem, there are also solutions to dealing with the problems caused by a drought. Scientists and engineers design new technologies to help locate and save water. Community leaders and government officials help make plans for better water management in order to ensure everyone gets the water they need, even during drought conditions.

By learning about the challenges we face and recognizing how essential water is to our lives, you can help. Every time you turn off the tap while brushing your teeth or choose plants for your garden that need less water, you are helping!

5 /
famous droughts in history

the dust bowl

JOURNEY back with us to the 1930s, when a strange thing began happening across the fields of the United States: The ground literally turned to sand, and clouds of dust swirled through the air for years. Hundreds of miles of farmland turned into deserts! It may sound like a story from a movie, but the Dust Bowl was all too real. Let's travel back in time to the Dust Bowl to learn the cause of this amazing event and what it was like to live through it.

The Setting

Once upon a time, in the central part of the United States, there were huge areas of land called the Great

Plains. These plains were covered with grass and home to many farms where families grew crops like wheat and corn. The soil was rich, the grass was green, and the land stretched on forever under the big, blue sky.

The Change

In the late 1920s, farmers thought they hit the jackpot. The prices for wheat were high, and new farming equipment made it easier to plant more and more crops. So, they plowed up millions of acres of natural grassland to plant wheat. But here's the twist: by doing so, they removed the deep-rooted grasses that held the soil in place.

Then, during the 1930s, a terrible drought struck. No rain fell for years, and the once fertile soil turned dry and dusty. Without the grasses to hold it down, the soil simply blew away with the wind. This was the beginning of the Dust Bowl.

Black Blizzards

Imagine waking up to a sky so dark that it looked like night, even in the middle of the day. These weren't regular storms but massive dust storms that people called "black blizzards." They could last for days, covering homes, farms, and entire towns with thick dust. Everything and everyone got coated in dirt.

Families stuffed rags under doors and taped windows, trying to keep the dust out of their homes. But it was no use; the dust got into everything, even food and water. Breathing became hard, and many people got sick from the "dust pneumonia."

Life During the Dust Bowl

Life during the Dust Bowl was tough. Many crops died, and without crops, farmers couldn't make money. Families faced hunger and poverty. Some people gave up their farms and moved to other states, hoping for a better life. They traveled long distances, often in old cars packed with all their belongings, not knowing what awaited them.

Children like you had to adapt to new homes and new schools, often facing challenges and uncertainty. Imagine having to start over, make new friends, and go to a new school in a completely different place!

Learning and Growing Stronger

· · ·

The Dust Bowl taught everyone a big lesson about taking care of the land. Farmers learned more about how to prevent soil erosion by using better farming techniques, like crop rotation and planting trees as windbreaks. These methods helped the soil stay healthy and in place, even during dry or windy conditions.

Scientists and the government started working together to create laws and practices to protect the environment and ensure that such a disaster would not happen again. They realized the importance of respecting and understanding nature.

The Legacy of the Dust Bowl

The story of the Dust Bowl is a reminder of how humans and nature are deeply connected. It shows us that our actions have consequences and that taking care of the Earth is important for everyone's future.

Today, we can learn from the past by being mindful of how we use natural resources and how we treat our planet. Each of us can make a difference, even with small actions like recycling, conserving water, and learning more about the environment.

Carry the Message Forward

As you go about your day, remember the tale of the Dust Bowl. It's a story of hardship but also of hope and recovery. It teaches us that even during the toughest times, people can come together, learn, and create a better world for tomorrow.

Keep asking questions, exploring the world, and thinking about how you can help take care of our planet. Every little bit helps, and who knows? Maybe you'll be the one to make a big difference. Keep being curious, and keep on adventuring!

the 2011 east africa drought

Come with me to East Africa, a stunningly beautiful place that suffered a great ordeal in 2011. This was not just any ordeal. This was an intense drought: one of the most severe droughts on record. Its destructive force quickly affected millions of people and animals and reminded all of us about our planet and how we divide up its gifts.

When the Rains Didn't Come

In 2011, the countries of Somalia, Ethiopia, and Kenya in East Africa were expecting their seasonal rains to start in October the previous year and again in the spring. These rains are crucial because they help grow the crops that feed the people and their livestock. But that year, the rains were late and much lighter than usual. Imagine waiting for a bus that never arrives—that's how the people felt waiting for the rain.

The Land and Its People

East Africa is a region of incredible landscapes, from vast savannas to high mountains. Many people here live as farmers or herders, relying on the land to feed their cattle, goats, and sheep. When the rains failed, the rivers began to dry up, and the grasslands turned to dust. Without water and pasture, animals started to die, and soon, the people began to fear for their own survival.

. . .

The Growing Crisis

As the drought continued, crops failed, and food became scarce. Water holes dried up, and people had to walk longer distances to find water. Imagine having to walk several hours just to fill a bucket of water for your family! It wasn't just hard; it was dangerous, too, because the region was also facing conflicts that made these journeys risky.

The Children of the Drought

For kids in East Africa, the drought meant changes in many parts of their lives. Many schools closed because there was not enough water or because teachers couldn't reach the schools. With families moving in search of water, many children had to leave their friends and homes behind. They also had to take on more responsibilities, like helping their families collect water or care for their younger siblings.

The World Responds

· · ·

When pictures and stories of the drought and its effects reached other parts of the world, many countries and organizations decided to help. They sent food, water, and medicine to help the people in East Africa. Aid workers from all over the world came to set up camps where people could come for food, water, and a safe place to stay. This global effort showed how, when people work together, they can help ease each other's suffering.

Lessons for the Future

The 2011 drought taught everyone a lot about how to better prepare for future challenges. Governments and organizations learned how important it is to have plans in place to deal with emergencies. They started projects to build better water storage systems, like dams and wells, so that people would have water even when the rains were late. They also worked on peace efforts, so that aid could reach those who needed it most without danger.

Green Shoots of Recovery

· · ·

Over time, the rains returned, and with them, hope. People began to rebuild their lives, crops began to grow again, and children went back to school. The wildlife that had suffered during the drought began to return, and the natural beauty of East Africa began to bloom once more.

australia's millennium drought

Come with me to a land down under, to the country of Australia. Starting in 1997, this proud nation was plunged into adversity which would last until 2009 known as the Millennium Drought. This dry spell wasn't just any old dry spell and was the worst drought experience by the hearty and adventurous people of Australia. Let's take a look at how the drought played out and how it affected the people and the land.

The Sunburnt Country

Australia, known for its vast outback, beautiful beaches, and bustling cities, is no stranger to dry weather. But the Millennium Drought was different. It was longer and harsher than anything people had seen in generations. Farms, rivers, and even big city water supplies felt the pinch as the skies stayed clear and the land turned dusty.

. . .

When the Rivers Run Low

In Australia, rivers are the lifelines. During the drought, these rivers carried less water. The mighty Murray-Darling Basin, which is a huge river system that lots of farmers depend on, was especially hard hit. Water levels dropped so low that patches of riverbed that hadn't been seen in decades were suddenly exposed.

Farms and Farmers

Imagine being a farmer, waiting and hoping for rain that never comes. For Australian farmers, the drought meant tough decisions. Water is needed not just for crops, but for cattle and sheep too. Many farmers had to sell animals they couldn't afford to water, or watch their crops fail, which meant less food to sell and less money to bring home.

Cities Feel the Heat

. . .

It wasn't just the countryside that felt the drought's sting; cities struggled too. In places like Melbourne and Sydney, water restrictions were put in place. People couldn't wash their cars with a hose or water their gardens at just any time. These rules helped make sure there was enough water for everyone to drink and bathe.

A Country Changes

As the drought wore on, everyone had to adapt. Gardens changed from green lawns to drought-resistant plants. Farmers learned new ways to conserve water, like using drip irrigation, which sends water directly to the roots of plants, where it's needed most.

Schools and communities started teaching more about how to save water, and even the youngest kids learned to turn off the tap while brushing their teeth.

Innovations and Ideas

· · ·

With challenges come innovations. Australians got creative, finding new ways to save and reuse water. New technology helped predict weather patterns better, and desalination plants, which turn seawater into fresh water, were built. These efforts weren't just about getting through the drought; they were about preparing for the future.

The Drought Breaks

Finally, in late 2009, the rains came. Rivers flowed, dams filled up, and dried-up grasslands turned green again. But the lessons of the Millennium Drought stayed. People continued to use water wisely, remembering the dry years and knowing they could come again.

A Story of Resilience

The tale of Australia's Millennium Drought is an inspiring one. It is a story of how people can deal with change, innovate, and together meet the challenge of adversity. It is a powerful reminder that we cannot control the climate, but we can control our response to it.

6 /
how people fight against drought

water conservation methods

EVERY TIME you turn on a tap, you're using up one of Earth's most valuable resources. Water is absolutely necessary for life, but it's easy to forget that it isn't in endless supply. Today, we're going to take a look at some incredible ways people all over the world are conserving water, both at home and on farms. So, let's get to it and discover all the amazing strategies you can use to help save water!

Water Wizards at Home

Saving water at home is easier than you might think, and it starts right where you live! Whether you're brushing your teeth or washing dishes, there's always a way to be a water wizard.

- Turn It Off: Did you know a running faucet can use about 2 gallons of water per minute? By turning off the tap while brushing your teeth or scrubbing dishes, you save a ton of water! Just imagine, if you save even 1 gallon each time, over a year, that adds up to a lot of water for the planet.

- Shower Power: Showers can be water guzzlers. By taking shorter showers, you can save water without even thinking about it. There are also cool gadgets called low-flow showerheads that use less water but still make you feel like you're under a waterfall!

- Fix those Drips: A leaky faucet that drips once per second can waste more than 3,000 gallons per year. That's enough water for a lot of showers or loads of laundry! Fixing leaks is like being a detective; find those drips and stop them in their tracks.

· · ·

- Full Loads Only: Running your washing machine or dishwasher only when they're full means you use less water and energy. It's like making every drop of water count by doing as much work as possible.

Farm Fresh Water-Saving

Farms need a lot of water to grow food, but farmers are becoming super savvy about saving water. Here's how they're doing it:

- Drip Drop: Drip irrigation is a super cool system that delivers water right to the roots of plants, where it's needed most. This means less water is wasted, and plants get just the right amount to drink.

- Mulch Magic: Farmers use mulch to cover the soil around their plants. Mulch keeps the soil moist by reducing evaporation. It's like giving the soil a little protective blanket.

. . .

- Choose Smart Crops: Some plants need less water than others. Farmers can choose crops that are suited to the local climate, which means they naturally need less water to grow.

- Water Scheduling: By watering crops at the best times of the day, like early morning or late evening, farmers can reduce water loss to evaporation. It's all about timing!

Tech to the Rescue

With the help of technology, saving water gets even easier. There are gadgets and apps that can tell you how much water you're using and even alert you if there's a leak. Imagine having a smart home that helps you save water every day!

Community Water Heroes

Water conservation isn't just something you do alone; entire communities can come together to save water.

Some neighborhoods have community gardens with drought-resistant plants, or they organize workshops to teach everyone how to be water-wise.

technological innovations like drought-resistant crops

Consider for a moment, drought-resistant crops. That's right, crops that are just as cool as they sound. They're not just your typical plants. They're more like the super-heroes of plants. They only need about a fourth of the water other plants need. Well, why in the world would anyone need plants like that? Because then you can grow food! Food, of course. But where would you need to grow food like that? Somewhere where it doesn't rain very often at all.

Meet the Super Plants

Drought-resistant crops are plants that have been specially developed to grow in dry conditions. Scientists use cool techniques like genetic engineering and selective breeding to create these plants. This means they pick the best traits from different plants—like the ability to grow with less water—and combine them to make a super plant.

. . .

For example, imagine you could take the speed of a cheetah and the strength of an elephant and combine them into one awesome animal. That's kind of what scientists are doing with these plants!

How Do These Plants Work?

These super plants have some special features that help them survive when water is scarce. Here are a few:

- Deep Roots: Some drought-resistant crops have really deep roots that can reach water buried far below the surface. It's like having a long straw that can reach the last drop at the bottom of a milkshake glass.

- Waxy Leaves: Other plants might have waxy leaves that help them hold onto moisture and prevent water from evaporating. These leaves are like tiny umbrellas keeping the water safe and sound.

- Grow Slow, Save Water: Some of these plants grow slower on purpose. By taking their time, they don't use up water too quickly, which is pretty smart if you think about it.

Why Are These Plants So Important?

In many parts of the world, water is becoming more precious than gold. Having plants that need less water means farmers can grow food even in places where it's dry. This helps make sure that everyone, no matter where they live, can have enough food to eat.

Plus, using less water for farming means there's more water left for other things like drinking and keeping rivers and lakes full. It's all about sharing the water wisely.

Super Plants in Action

Let's take a trip around the world to see these plants in action:

. . .

- In Africa: Farmers are growing drought-resistant maize, which helps them produce more food even when there's hardly any rain.

- In India: Millet and sorghum are popular because they can handle the hot, dry weather and still make plenty of seeds for eating.

- In the United States: Scientists are working on drought-resistant soybeans and wheat, helping farmers keep up with everyone's needs for bread, cereal, and more.

The Future of Farming

With climate change making the weather more unpredictable, these drought-resistant crops are becoming superstars in the farming world. They are part of what many people call "sustainable farming," which means farming in a way that can keep going for a long time without running out of resources.

. . .

In the future, we might see even more types of these plants, and farmers will have more tools to help them grow food in tough conditions. Who knows? Maybe one day you'll help invent a new kind of super plant!

Growing Forward

Every time you learn about how our world works—like how plants can be tweaked to save water—you're getting smarter about how to take care of our planet. These drought-resistant crops are just one of the many amazing ways people are working to make sure we all have enough food and water.

Remember, every bit of knowledge helps, and who knows? Maybe you'll be the one to come up with a new solution to help the world. So keep learning, keep asking questions, and keep dreaming about how you can be part of making our world a better place. Let's grow a greener, more water-wise world together! Keep exploring, young scientists!

community projects and laws to save water

Special projects and particular rules some communities have put in place to help save water. Think of it as being on a team; everybody has a part to play in being smart with water-use . It looks like it's time for you to get your water wings on so we can see what some places do for saving water and really make a splash!

Water Saving Starts with Us

Water is super important, right? We need it to drink, wash, and grow our food. But sometimes, there isn't enough to go around. That's when communities need to get creative and work together to make sure there's enough water for everyone.

Cool Community Projects

All around the world, people are starting projects to help save water. Here are some neat ways communities are doing their part:

. . .

- Rainwater Harvesting: Some neighborhoods install systems to catch rainwater. This water can be used for watering gardens or flushing toilets. Imagine collecting raindrops in a giant bucket and then using that water to keep plants happy!

- Community Gardens with Drought-Resistant Plants: Instead of each person watering their own garden, communities sometimes create a big garden where everyone can help grow fruits and veggies. By using plants that don't need much water, they save heaps of water!

- Educational Programs: Schools and community centers often host workshops to teach people, just like you, how to save water at home. Learning things like turning off the tap while brushing your teeth really adds up.

Laws to Keep the Water Flowing

Sometimes, to make sure there's enough water for everyone, places need to make rules about how water can be used. These laws help everyone understand how important it is to save water.

- Water Restrictions: In some areas, especially during very dry months, there might be rules about when you can water your lawn or wash your car. This helps make sure there's enough water for more important things like drinking and cooking.

- Building Codes for Water Efficiency: New houses and buildings sometimes have to include things like low-flow toilets and showerheads that use less water. This means new homes are already set up to save water!

- Fines for Wasting Water: In some places, if you use way too much water or you're not following the water-saving rules, you might have to pay a fine. It's like a reminder to everyone to stick to the rules so there's enough water to go around.

Stories of Success

·   ·   ·

Let's look at some real-life examples of how these projects and laws have helped communities:

- In one small town, after they started catching rainwater, they had enough extra water to fill a small swimming pool every month! That's a lot of water saved just by collecting rain.

- In another community, after the school started teaching kids about water conservation, the whole town reduced its water use by 10%. That's like if every person used 10 fewer buckets of water each month!

How You Can Get Involved

You might be wondering, "What can I do to help save water?" Well, there are lots of ways you can make a difference, even as a kid!

- Become a Water Ambassador: Learn all you can about saving water and teach your friends and family what you've learned. You could make posters or give a little talk at your school.

- Participate in Community Clean-Ups: Help keep local rivers and lakes clean by joining in community clean-up days. A clean waterway helps keep the water healthy, which is good for everyone.

- Start a Water-Saving Project at Home: With your family, try catching some rainwater or setting up a system to reuse water from your home. Every little project helps!

7 /
what can you do to help?

tips for conserving water daily

DID you know how much water we use every day? Everything from brushing your teeth to watering your garden costs water. That's right! However, there are some amazing little things we can do every day to save water. Okay, let's do some water saving magic with the following fun and easy tips for preserving our planet's most precious resource for all of us!

Start the Day Saving Water

Morning routines are perfect for saving water. Here's how you can make a splash by using less:

- Brushing Time: When you brush your teeth, turn off the tap until it's time to rinse. Just imagine, if you save a few cups of water every time, that adds up to a whole lot of water by the end of the year!

- Short Showers: Challenge yourself to take shorter showers. Try to finish before your favorite song ends. Not only will you save water, but you'll also have extra time to do fun stuff.

. . .

Wise Water in the Kitchen

The kitchen is another water hotspot. But don't worry, there are simple ways to turn it into a water-saving zone:

- Dishwasher Savvy: If you have a dishwasher, make sure it's full before you run it. Dishwashers can use less water than washing dishes by hand if you do it right.
    - Filling the Kettle: Love hot cocoa? When you fill the kettle, use only as much water as you need. This saves water and energy (plus, your drink will be ready faster!).

Learning with Laundry

Doing laundry might sound boring, but it can be a great way to save water:

- Full Loads: Just like the dishwasher, washing machines should be full before you start them. This means you do fewer loads and save water.
    - Cool Choices: Using cold water for washing can save water and energy. It's a win-win!

. . .

Become a Garden Guru

Gardens love water, but you don't have to use a lot to keep them happy:

- Morning Watering: Water your plants early in the morning or late in the evening. Less water will evaporate this way compared to the hot midday sun.
    - Catch Rain: Set up a rain barrel to catch water when it rains. Use this water for your plants. They don't mind if it's a bit muddy!

Power in the Bathroom

The bathroom uses a lot of water, but there are quick fixes to help reduce that amount:

- Leak Patrol: Keep an ear out for dripping taps or running toilets. These leaks can waste a lot of water. Fixing them can be a fun detective game – find that drip, stop that leak!

- Flush Facts: Did you know older toilets use more water? If you have an older toilet, try putting a filled water bottle in the tank to reduce the amount of water used per flush. Just make sure it doesn't affect flushing!

Sharing Your Water-Saving Super Skills

Saving water is more fun when you do it with friends and family:

- Teach Others: Share your water-saving tips with friends at school. Maybe you could make posters or do a presentation to spread the word.

- Family Challenge: Start a family challenge to see who can save the most water. You can even have little rewards like choosing what's for dinner!

fun water-saving activities and challenges

Are you ready to have a great time and save the planet? We're here to walk you through some absolutely amazing activities and challenges. All of these activities help us save water and are also buckets of fun! Save water at home, at school, and out and about in your community and city. Saving water is a super-fun adventure and we can't wait to get started!

Water Detective Mission

What You Need:
- A notebook
- A pencil
- A watch or timer

How to Play:

Become a water detective for a day! Your mission is to find out where your home might be using more water than it needs. Check all the faucets, showers, and toilets for leaks. Time how long you run the water to brush your teeth or wash dishes. Write down what you find and show your family how they could save water based on your detective work. Maybe you'll find a leaky faucet that's been wasting water without anyone knowing!

Shower Song Challenge

. . .

What You Need:
- A playlist of your favorite songs

How to Play:

Pick one of your favorite songs that lasts about three to five minutes. Start the song when you begin your shower, and try to finish before the song ends. This challenge makes saving water fun and musical! You can even make it a family competition to see who can consistently take the shortest showers (but still get clean, of course!).

Bucket Brigade Race

What You Need:
- A couple of buckets
- A stopwatch

How to Play:

This game is perfect for a sunny day outside. Set up a start line and a finish line in your yard or at a park. Fill a bucket with water at the start line. The goal is to carry the bucket to the finish line without spilling any water. You can race against time or against friends. This game teaches you how important it is to handle water carefully —every drop counts!

Drip Drop Savings

What You Need:
- A dripping faucet (if you have one that needs fixing)
- A large bowl
- A measuring cup

How to Play:
Place the bowl under the dripping faucet and collect the water for an hour. Measure how much water was wasted. Then, fix the faucet (with help from an adult) and do the same thing, showing how no water is wasted anymore. This activity visually shows how fixing a small drip can save a lot of water!

Water-Wise Gardening

What You Need:
- Seeds of plants that require little water

- Soil
- Pots or a garden patch

How to Play:

Start a water-wise garden by planting drought-resistant plants or vegetables. Research with an adult which plants are best for your area. As you take care of your garden, keep a diary of how much water you use. Try different methods, like mulching or using a watering can instead of a hose, to see how you can grow plants with minimal water.

Classroom Water Challenge

What You Need:
- Your classmates and teacher
- A chart to track progress

How to Play:

Organize a month-long water-saving challenge at your school. Each class tracks the water they save, from drinking water wisely to ensuring taps are fully turned off. At the end of the month, see which class saved the most water. This can be a great way to raise awareness and start a conversation about water conservation in your school.

Water-Saving Science Fair

What You Need:
- Science fair materials
- Ideas for water conservation projects

How to Play:

Host a science fair where the main theme is water conservation. You and your friends can come up with projects that showcase different ways to save or recycle water. From demonstrating how different soils retain water to building models of rainwater harvesting systems, the possibilities are endless!

how to spread awareness about the importance of water conservation

Convincing others to care for water storage can be just as exciting as learning about it. So, how do you encourage others to save water? Today, you will learn how to advocate for water storage for all. It will be fun to spread the word and make a splash.

Become a Water Wise Whisperer

First things first: to spread awareness, you need to know your stuff! You've learned lots of cool water-saving tips, like turning off the tap while brushing your teeth and taking shorter showers. Now, it's your turn to be the teacher. Start by telling your family and friends what you know. You can even make it fun by showing them exactly how they can save water with little changes at home.

Create Cool Content

One of the best ways to spread the word is by creating eye-catching posters or digital content. Think about making bright, colorful posters to hang in your school hallways or a fun video to share on social media (with a parent's help, of course!). You could illustrate how much water people can save with simple actions, like fixing leaks or using a watering can instead of a hose in the garden.

. . .

School Projects and Presentations

School is a great place to raise awareness about water conservation. You could do a project or presentation for your class about why water is precious and how everyone can help save it. Use clear examples and maybe even a little experiment, like showing how much water a dripping tap wastes in an hour. It's a surefire way to make your classmates think twice about leaving the tap running!

Community Champions

Getting your whole community involved can make a big difference. How about organizing a water-saving workshop with local experts? Or setting up a booth at a community fair where you hand out water-saving tips and stickers? You could also talk to local businesses about putting up signs in their restrooms reminding people to use water wisely.

Fun Competitions

. . .

Everyone loves a challenge, especially if there are prizes involved. Organize a water-saving challenge at your school or in your neighborhood. Who can come up with the most creative way to save water? Or who can reduce their household water use the most? Challenges like these can really get people excited about making a difference.

Write About It

If you enjoy writing, you could write articles or blog posts about the importance of water conservation. Share stories about what people around the world are doing to save water. You could even interview water conservation experts and share their insights. Local newspapers and websites might be interested in publishing your work, spreading the message even further.

Social Media Sharing

With the help of an adult, use social media to spread the word even wider. Quick tips, interesting water facts, or pictures of your water conservation efforts can inspire others to join in. Remember, the more people see how important and easy it is to save water, the more they're likely to start doing it themselves.

Lead by Example

The best way to inspire others is by being a great example. Let people see you practicing what you preach. If you're always looking for ways to use less water and talking about why it's important, people will notice. They might even start asking you for tips on how they can save water too!

Celebrate Water!

Finally, celebrate water in all its glory! Participate in or organize events on important days like World Water Day. These are perfect opportunities to celebrate all the ways water makes life on Earth possible. Plus, it's a great time to remind everyone about the importance of conserving this precious resource.

conclusion

The Journey Begins with Understanding

Our journey started with understanding what droughts are and how they affect our planet. We learned that droughts are not just about dry land and thirsty plants, but they also impact everything from the water in our taps to the food on our plates. Whether it's the water cycle or the different types of droughts, we now know how deeply water is connected to everything we do.

Everyday Heroes Saving Water

Then, we rolled up our sleeves and looked at how we can save water in our daily lives. From turning off the tap while brushing our teeth to taking shorter showers, every small action adds up to big savings on water. We also discovered how fixing a simple leak can save thousands of gallons of water each year. Imagine all the other things that water could do!

Water Wizards at Work

We didn't stop there! We learned about the amazing technology and smart farming practices that help save water on a bigger scale. Drought-resistant crops and efficient irrigation systems show us how innovation can make a huge difference. By choosing plants that need less water and using clever gadgets to keep soil moist, farmers are helping to make sure there's enough water to go around.

Community Champions

We also saw how entire communities come together to protect their water sources. From rainwater harvesting systems to community gardens, people everywhere are finding ways to be more water-wise. We learned that when communities work together, they can overcome even the biggest challenges, like the Millennium Drought in Australia or the water crisis in East Africa.

Spreading the Word

One of the most exciting things we discovered is that anyone, no matter how young, can help spread the word about water conservation. By making posters, giving presentations, or just talking to friends and family, you can inspire others to start saving water too. Every conversation you start can lead to new ideas and actions that help keep our water clean and plentiful.

A World of Water Warriors

Through all these discoveries, we've seen how every one of us can be a water warrior. It doesn't matter if you're at home, at school, or out in the community; there are always opportunities to make a difference. And remember, being a water saver not only helps our planet —it makes us part of a global team working together for a better future.

Why Your Actions Matter

Every day, you make choices that affect how much water you use. Whether it's choosing a short shower instead of a bath or turning off the tap while you brush your teeth, these choices add up. By being careful with water, you help make sure there's enough to go around—for people, plants, and animals.

The Power of One Becomes the Power of Many

When you start saving water, you also start a wave of change. Imagine if you inspire your family to try saving water too. Then maybe they inspire their friends, and those friends inspire more friends. Before you know it, your one small change is making a big difference in your community!

Everyday Ways to Be a Water Saver

Here are some easy ways you can be proactive about water conservation every single day:

- Be a Leak Detective: Keep an eye out for leaks at home—from dripping taps to running toilets. Letting an adult know about a leak can save gallons of water.

- Smart Sipping: Only pour the amount of water you'll actually drink. If you see half-full water bottles lying around after a sports game or a picnic, think about ways to use that leftover water, like watering plants.

- Reuse and Recycle Water: Got water left over from washing fruits and veggies? Use it to water house plants. It's a great way to recycle water.

- Spread the Word: Use your voice to teach others about saving water. Whether it's during a school project, at a community meeting, or even online, sharing what you know helps others become water savers too.

School and Community Initiatives

Getting involved in school or community projects can amplify your impact:

- Start a Water Watchers Club: Gather a group of friends at school who are interested in water conservation and start a club. You can organize events, create informative posters, and even challenge other classes to save water.

- Participate in Community Clean-Ups: Join local efforts to clean up rivers, lakes, and beaches. Keeping water bodies clean helps protect the environment and conserve water.

- Advocate for Change: Encourage your school or community center to install water-efficient toilets, faucets, and sprinklers. Sometimes, just starting the conversation can lead to big changes.

Celebrate Your Achievements

Every time you take a step to save water, give yourself a pat on the back. It's important to celebrate your efforts and keep yourself motivated. Maybe keep a journal of all the ways you've helped save water, or create a chart to track your family's water-saving efforts each month.

Why Your Future Depends on Water

Remember, water isn't just important now—it will be crucial in the future too. By learning to save water today, you're helping ensure that there's enough water for you and future generations. You're not just saving water; you're saving habitats, helping communities thrive, and protecting the earth.

We're All in This Together

You're part of a global team of young people who care about our planet. Every action you take to save water joins with the actions of millions of others around the world who are just as committed to making a difference. Together, you're not just water savers; you're planet protectors.

Keep the Wave Rolling

So, what's next? Keep learning, keep teaching, and keep acting. Every little thing you learn about water can spark big ideas for how to save it. And every person you teach how to save water helps spread the wave. You have the power to change the world, one drop at a time.

You're already doing so much great work, and I can't wait to see how you continue to grow as a water hero. Keep it up, keep seeking new ideas, and remember— every little bit counts. You're saving the planet one drip at a time. Let's keep it up, keep learning, and make sure our world stays healthy and hydrated.

glossary

Water Cycle

This is the journey that water takes as it moves around Earth in different forms, from rivers to clouds to rain and back again. It has several stages:

- Evaporation: When the sun heats up water in rivers, lakes, or oceans, and it turns into vapor or steam.

- Condensation: When the water vapor cools down and changes back into liquid, forming clouds.

- Precipitation: When water falls from the sky as rain, snow, sleet, or hail.

- Collection: When the water that falls from the sky ends up back in lakes, rivers, and oceans, and the cycle starts all over.

Drought

This is a long period without rain, which can lead to a shortage of water. There are a few types of droughts:

- Meteorological Drought: When dry weather patterns dominate an area.

- Agricultural Drought: When there isn't enough water for crops to grow.

- Hydrological Drought: When the water levels in rivers and lakes are lower than usual.

- Socioeconomic Drought: When the demand for water is greater than the supply, affecting people and the economy.

Conservation

This means protecting something and using it wisely. Water conservation involves using less water and finding ways to use water more efficiently to make sure we have enough for the future.

Aquifer

This is an underground layer of rock or sand that can hold water. People often get drinking water from aquifers by drilling wells.

Watershed

This is an area of land that drains all the streams and rainfall to a common outlet like a reservoir, mouth of a bay, or any point along a stream channel. It's like a big bowl that catches all the water that falls into it.

Irrigation

This is when people artificially bring water to crops by channeling it from rivers, lakes, or reservoirs. It helps farmers grow crops in areas where there isn't enough rain.

Low-Flow Fixtures

These are special devices that use less water than normal ones. For example, low-flow showerheads and faucets reduce the amount of water that comes out but still get you clean or do the job well.

Rainwater Harvesting

This is when you collect rainwater on your roof or in a field from rain or snow, which can then be used for things like watering plants, flushing toilets, or even washing cars. It's a great way to make use of water that would otherwise go down the drain.

Gray Water

This is water that has been used in homes but not for anything involving waste. For example, water from sinks, showers, or washing machines can be reused for watering gardens or lawns, which is a smart way to recycle water.

Xeriscaping

This is a way of landscaping that reduces or eliminates the need for supplemental water from irrigation. It involves using plants that are native to the area and can survive with natural amounts of rainfall, and it's super helpful in dry regions.

Evapotranspiration

This is the process by which water is transferred from the land to the atmosphere by evaporation from soil and other surfaces and by transpiration from plants. It's how plants "breathe" and release water vapor back into the air.

Water Footprint

This is the total amount of fresh water that is used to produce the goods and services consumed by an individual or community. It helps us understand the impact our lifestyle has on global water resources.

Permeable Surfaces

These are materials that allow liquids or gases to pass through them. Permeable paving materials in your garden, like certain types of bricks or gravel, let rainwater soak into the ground, reducing runoff and helping to recharge aquifers.

Water-Efficient

This term is used to describe products or systems that use less water to perform as well or better than standard products. These can include toilets, showerheads, faucets, and irrigation systems designed to conserve water.

activities and resources

games and quizzes to reinforce learning

Let's Play: Games and Quizzes to Make Water Conservation Fun

Water Drop Relay

How to Play:

This game needs at least two teams with equal numbers of players. Each team gets a bucket of water and an empty bucket placed several feet away. The challenge? Transfer as much water as possible from one bucket to the other using only a sponge! This game teaches about the careful handling of water and how important it is to avoid wasting it.

- Materials Needed:
    - Two large buckets per team
    - Sponges
    - Water

- Objective:

Learn the importance of water conservation through careful handling and the challenge of transporting water without spills.

Thirsty Word Search

Create a word search puzzle using key terms from our water conservation lessons, like "aquifer," "drought," "evaporation," and more. Finding each word can trigger a discussion about its importance and how it fits into the bigger picture of water conservation.

- Materials Needed:
    - Printed word search grids
    - Pens or pencils

- Objective:

Reinforce key vocabulary related to water conservation and understand their meanings through play.

DIY Water Cycle Board Game

Design your own board game based on the water cycle. Players can move around the board, landing on spaces that require them to answer questions correctly about the water cycle to move forward. Add challenges like 'lose a turn' for landing on a pollution space or 'move ahead' for rainwater harvesting.

- Materials Needed:
    - Cardboard or a large poster for the board
    - Markers and decorations
    - Dice
    - Player tokens

- Objective:

Educate players about the water cycle's stages and the impact of human activities on water resources in a fun, interactive way.

Leak Fix Flip

In this timed challenge, players race against the clock to 'fix' leaks around a model home setup. Use a dollhouse or draw a home layout on cardboard. Place markers where leaks are commonly found (like under sinks and near washing machines), and players must find and 'fix' the leaks with tape or pretend tools.

- Materials Needed:
    - A model home setup (dollhouse or cardboard)
    - Timer
    - Pretend tools or tape

- Objective:
    Teach about common household leaks and the importance of fixing them quickly to conserve water.

Water Wise Quiz Show

Host a quiz show where kids answer questions about water conservation. Include multiple-choice questions, true/false, and challenge questions for extra points. Questions can range from daily water-saving tips to facts about global water usage.

- Materials Needed:
    - List of questions and answers
    - Buzzer or bell for each participant
    - Scoreboard

- Objective:
    Test and reinforce knowledge about water conservation in a fun, competitive setting.

The Great Water Journey Challenge

This activity involves creating a map or course that represents the water cycle. Participants complete tasks at each 'station' related to different aspects of the water cycle and water conservation efforts, such as 'rain dance', 'evaporation hopscotch', or 'clean the river' picking up trash.

- Materials Needed:
    - Stations set up around a large space or playground
    - Props for each station (e.g., water, cups, trash items)
    - Instructions for each station

- Objective:
    Combine physical activity with learning about the water cycle and conservation efforts.

Keep the Fun Flowing

But remember, each game you play and each quiz you take brings you one step closer to understanding how rare and important water is and what you can do to conserve it. These games, quizzes and pictures aren't just for fun—they're for making you a better water warrior!

So keep playing, keep learning, keep caring and keep conserving. You're not only helping save water; you're making sure it can be enjoyed by everyone today and tomorrow. Grab your sponges, get your pencils ready and prepare to flex your creative muscles. Saving water is now the most fun part of your day and you should be ready to tackle it like a real water warrior! You're saving our planet, game by game. Keep up the great work!

diy experiments related to water conservation

Experiment 1: The Drip Detective

Objective: Learn how much water a dripping faucet can waste.

Materials Needed:
- A sink with a faucet that drips
- A measuring cup or a container with measurement markings
- A stopwatch or clock
- A notebook and pen for recording data

Instructions:
1. Place the measuring cup under the dripping faucet.
2. Use the stopwatch to time 30 minutes.
3. After 30 minutes, check how much water has collected in the cup.
4. Record the amount of water in your notebook.
5. Calculate how much water would drip in 24 hours

by multiplying the amount collected by 48 (since 30 minutes is 1/48th of a day).

Discussion:

Talk about how much water can be wasted by a simple drip over a week, a month, or even a year! This experiment helps show why it's important to fix leaks promptly.

Experiment 2: The Shower Bucket Challenge

Objective: See how much water is used during a typical shower.

Materials Needed:

- A bucket (big enough to fit under your shower head)
- A stopwatch or timer
- A measuring jug

Instructions:

1. Place the bucket under the shower head.

2. Turn on the shower to the usual pressure you use, and time how long it takes to fill the bucket.

3. Measure the volume of water in the bucket using the jug.

4. Record your findings and calculate how much

water you use in a full-length shower (if one bucket fills in 1 minute, and you shower for 5 minutes, multiply the volume by 5).

Discussion:

Discuss how changing shower habits or installing water-efficient showerheads can reduce water use.

Experiment 3: Soil Moisture Test

Objective: Find out how different soils hold water and discuss the best types of soil for conserving water in gardens.

Materials Needed:

- Samples of different types of soil (sand, clay, potting soil, etc.)
- Several small containers
- Water
- A notebook for observations

Instructions:

1. Fill each container with a different type of soil.
2. Slowly pour the same amount of water into each container.
3. Observe how the water is absorbed by the soil.
4. Record which types of soil retain water longer.

Discussion:

Talk about how using the right type of soil in your garden can help conserve water. This is especially important in areas that experience droughts.

Experiment 4: Evaporation Exploration

Objective: Understand how factors like heat and air movement affect water evaporation.

Materials Needed:
- Two shallow dishes or pans
- Water
- A sunny spot
- A fan (optional)

Instructions:
1. Fill both dishes with an equal amount of water.
2. Place one dish in a sunny spot and the other in the same spot but with a fan blowing lightly over it.
3. Observe and record the level of water in each dish every hour for several hours.
4. Note which dish loses water faster.

Discussion:

Discuss how the results could relate to saving water in your home or school. For instance, covering pools reduces evaporation, just like reducing air flow over water can.

Experiment 5: Plant Watering Techniques

Objective: Discover which watering method is most efficient for keeping plants hydrated.

Materials Needed:
- Two similar potted plants
- A watering can
- A spray bottle

Instructions:

1. Water one plant by pouring water directly onto the soil from the watering can.

2. Water the other plant with the spray bottle, misting the leaves and soil.

3. Do this once daily for a week, using the same amount of water for each plant.

4. Observe and record the health and soil moisture of each plant at the end of the week.

Discussion:

Talk about which method was more effective and why. Discuss how different watering methods can conserve water in agriculture and gardening.

By completing these experiments, you'll not only have fun but also learn valuable lessons about water conservation that you can share with others. Each experiment gives you a chance to see real-life science in action and makes you a better-informed guardian of our planet's water resources. So keep experimenting, keep learning, and remember, every drop counts! Let's make every experiment a step toward a more water-wise world!

a list of websites and books for further exploration

Wonderful Water Websites

1. Water Use It Wisely
   - What's Cool About It?: Offers tons of easy tips for saving water and fun games and tools designed just for kids.
   - Website: [Water Use It Wisely](http://www.wateruseitwisely.com/kids/)

2. The Water Project
   - What's Cool About It?: Provides detailed information on global water issues and how different communities are solving them.
   - Website: [The Water Project](https://thewaterproject.org/)

3. National Geographic Kids

- What's Cool About It?: Features exciting information about the environment, focusing on water and the animals that depend on it.

- Website: [National Geographic Kids](https://kids.nationalgeographic.com/)

4. EPA's WaterSense for Kids

- What's Cool About It?: Teaches about water conservation through interactive games and provides tips on how to save water at home.

- Website: [EPA WaterSense Kids](https://www.epa.gov/watersense/watersense-kids)

5. Project WET

- What's Cool About It?: Provides educational resources on water for students and teachers, including lesson plans and interactive learning tools.

- Website: [Project WET](http://www.projectwet.org/)

9 798330 614202